Returning Home to Your Catholic Faith

An Invitation

Sally L. Mews

Liguori
LIGUORI, MISSOURI

Imprimi Potest:
Richard Thibodeau, C.Ss.R.
Provincial, Denver Province
The Redemptorists

Published by Liguori Publications
Liguori, Missouri
www.liguori.org

Library of Congress Cataloging-in-Publication Data

Mews, Sally L.
    Returning home to your Catholic faith : an invitation / Sally L. Mews.—1st. ed.
        p. cm.
    ISBN 978-0-7648-1099-2 (pbk.)
    1. Ex-church members—Catholic Church. 2. Catholic Church—Membership. 3. Catholic Church—Doctrines. I. Title.

BX2347.8.E82M496 2003
282—dc22   2003054626

Printed in the United States of America
11 10   7 6

Contents

Foreword

Jesus loved to talk with people about their lives and to listen carefully to them. Often, as a result, they would find themselves having a whole new outlook on themselves, because he had made them feel valued and respected. As a result they found themselves having new hope about their lives. He never condemned anyone who opened their hearts to him or turned anybody away no matter what mistakes they revealed or confessed or how ordinary their lives were. One man, Zacchaeus, who encountered Jesus, had cheated many people in business. One woman, a Samaritan whom Jesus met at the town well, had been married five times and was living at that time with yet another man. Jesus found them worthy of his attention and so he took some time to spend with them. After their meetings with Jesus, their lives took on a whole new dimension of vitality and renewal.

Two persons who had believed in Jesus and then lost their faith when he was crucified carried their disappointment and grief with them as they took a journey to Emmaus on that first Easter Sunday afternoon. Their world had been turned upside down and fell in ruins around them. What they had hoped for—the arrival of a messiah—didn't happen. This stranger was Jesus whom they didn't recognize. He showed them how important it is to take a second look at things, for they aren't always what they seem (Lk 24:15–35). They opened the doors to their hearts and minds, and the world became a new place, a new creation. They were transformed and so was their world.

Most people who talked with Jesus were ordinary folks who felt a need to move beyond the superficial. They weren't satisfied with the way things were in their lives. Since the Second Vatican Council in the early 1960s the Catholic Church has recognized more and more that one's human development is an important aspect of one's growth in faith, love, and the ability to hope. All seekers have their "growing edges" where they experience God's invitation to take a new responsibility for their own decisions and choices and not simply follow the crowd. Sometimes these opportunities for growth occur when someone challenges us to "get real" and as a result we decide to take stock. Other times growth opportunities occur when we come to a realization on our own that there has to be another way. Sometimes renewal occurs because someone has come into our lives like the stranger in the Emmaus story, and we feel respected, valued, and energized to do something different.

Bernard Lonergan, S.J., the famous philosopher and theologian, called those moments "horizon changing moments." They are times when we no longer see the world as we have before. They are conversions. Some conversion experiences inspire changes in thinking, some inspire changes in feeling, and some changes in values. Someone or something has shifted our perspective. We find ourselves feeling what it is like to walk in someone else's shoes. We notice what we had been oblivious to. We realize that we can love more deeply than we have up to this point and we find ourselves relishing our new-found perceptions. God feels less like a stranger, and the world seems alive with God's warmth and encouragement. Our relationships are stronger and more resilient. They become more and more like the relationships of an independent adult who has a lot to give and is not afraid to receive.

The ministry of "Catholics Returning Home," which invites inactive Catholics to return home to their deeper selves and to the dynamic God who has always dwelled within the deepest part of their hearts, is based on the spirit of conversion and the renewal of relationships. Catholics Returning Home is an experience in grace and community which meets a person where he/she is with all of their unique history and says welcome home. A decision to participate in a Catholics Returning Home program is itself a turning point, a new moment of conversion in thinking, feeling, valuing as possible returnees begin to reclaim their spiritual heritage and make it more truly their own than it ever was before.

Part of a person's reclamation of the wholeness of her or his life and its heritage may well involve the expert assistance of a pastoral counselor who can help address any emotional or psychospiritual wounds incurred during one's journey in life up to that point. Such assistance could also help the transitional process of returning to the Church itself. A good resource for such assistance is the American Association of Pastoral Counselors. It may be reached at *www.aapc.org*. May the Lord of the journey to Emmaus walk with all who read *Returning Home to Your Catholic Faith*.

—WILLIAM J. MANSEAU, D. MIN.
FOUNDER AND PRESIDENT, EMMAUS INSTITUTE, INC.
NASHUA, NEW HAMPSHIRE

Chapter One

You Are Welcome and Missed

∼∽∼

Now all the tax collectors and sinners were coming near to listen to [Jesus]. And the Pharisees and the scribes were grumbling and saying, "This fellow welcomes sinners and eats with them."

So he told them this parable: "Which one of you, having a hundred sheep and losing one of them, does not leave the ninety-nine in the wilderness and go after the one that is lost until he finds it? When he has found it, he lays it on his shoulders and rejoices. And when he comes home, he calls together his friends, saying to them, 'Rejoice with me, for I have found my sheep that was lost.' Just so, I tell you, there will be more joy in heaven over one sinner who repents than over ninety-nine righteous persons who need no repentance.

"Or what woman having ten silver coins, if she loses one of them, does not light a lamp, sweep the house, and search carefully until she finds it? When she has found it, she calls together her friends and neighbors, saying, 'Rejoice with me, for I have found the coin that I had lost.' Just so, I tell you, there is joy in the presence of the angels of God over one sinner who repents."

LUKE 15:1–10

༺ঙ৯ঌ༻

H ave you drifted away from the Church and God? Have you stopped attending church or do you attend infrequently? Are you angry at the church or God? No matter how long you've been away for whatever reason, you're welcome to return. Your faith community misses you and is incomplete without you. As in the parable of Divine Mercy, Jesus, the Good Shepherd, is seeking you out and inviting you to return. The very angels in heaven are rejoicing over the prospect of your return.

Millions and millions of Catholics worldwide have stopped practicing their faith for various reasons. Some drift away during adolescence while searching for their own identity. Sadly, some have been hurt by people within the Church. Others find their lifestyles at odds with Church teaching. In the back of their minds many who have left the Church eventually want to return. However, many think they're not welcome and some even believe that they are excommunicated. Though these nonpracticing Catholics have separated themselves from their Catholic faith community, the reality is that they are always welcome to return home to the Catholic faith.

It doesn't matter if you've been away a few years or a lifetime; you can always reclaim your Catholic faith. It is your heritage and it belongs to you. If you have any doubt about your status, reread the parable of Divine Mercy at the beginning of this chapter. For most returning Catholics, it's simply a matter of returning to the sacraments, especially reconciliation. For others who have multiple marriages, the annulment process is available and can be worked through with the help of specially trained parish ministers. Nobody is beyond the mercy of God; therefore, no matter what your situation is, the Lord can help you work through it. Because outreach to nonpracticing Catholics is at the heart of the Church's mission, this effort is given top priority. Thus, many parishes have special outreach ministries for inviting nonpracticing Catholics to return.

Donna was in her mid forties when she first responded to an invitation to attend a Catholics Returning Home, an outreach ministry for nonpracticing Catholics. She had been away from the Church for over twenty years and really wasn't aware that she missed it except at funerals, holidays, and difficult times during her life. She was at a low point in her life because her mother was dying and she was being laid off from her job after more than fifteen years of service. She passed by her local parish a couple times a day going to and from work, and noticed that they put a sign out front inviting Catholics to "return home." Next, she saw an article in her local newspaper also inviting Catholics to return home to their local parish. On impulse, she attended Mass on Christmas day, and the priest and lector made announcements inviting non-practicing Catholics to a six-week program designed to help them return. This openness and welcome was a pleasant surprise to her because no one had ever personally invited her to return to the Catholic Church. Donna attended the six-week series and kept quiet throughout. She liked the series so much that she attended the same series again and gradually started talking within the group. Next, she joined the team and became one of the leaders in ministry to inactive Catholics. Years later, Donna remains active in her parish as a eucharistic minister in addition to serving in several other ministries.

Lynn was in her late sixties when she first attended a Catholics Returning Home program. She was a widow, poor and struggling to support herself. Her husband had been an alcoholic and her grown son was following the same path. Lynn was trying to deal with the emotional anguish and pain that arose from these family dynamics. Though she had been away from the Church since high school, her Catholic faith had been important to her, even as she let it fade into history. She hoped to return but she didn't know where to start. Her family of origin was alcoholic and abusive. In addition, her father had incestuous relationships with most of her sisters. In fact, she wasn't sure if her mother was really her mother at all; instead she believed that her oldest "sister" was really her natural mother. She believed she was the offspring of her father impregnating her oldest sister. Without a doubt Lynn had a very emotionally troubled and tangled life!

Despite the fact that religion wasn't important in her family of origin or in her marriage, Lynn always wanted the security and stability of belonging to the Catholic Church, even though she felt completely unworthy and confused about her status. She was overjoyed to be invited to a Catholics Returning Home program and to be welcomed back to the Catholic faith community. After returning to the Church, she eventually became comfortable enough to join a Catholic retirement assisted living community. Lynn feels privileged and grateful to live out her golden years in a peaceful, secure Catholic retirement community among like-minded folks where she is no longer isolated and alone.

A young couple in their early twenties had recently moved from Chicago to one of the suburbs and saw the signs and newspaper articles inviting them to a Catholics Returning Home program. Both were thrilled that the Catholic Church cared enough to invite them back. Both had sporadically attended religious education programs while growing up, but felt they were completely ignorant about even the basics of the Catholic faith. They wanted to learn more about the Catholic Church and become part of a stable, welcoming faith community.

It really doesn't matter how old you are or how many years you've been away from the Church. From young to old, all are welcome. Seniors frequently have more time in their lives to think about their relationships with God and others and to pursue recreational and spiritual enrichment activities. Younger and middle-aged people conversely have jam-packed lives and frequently their religion is put at the bottom of their list of priorities. However, parents with young children often reconnect with the Catholic Church to have their children baptized and catechized because they want the best for their offspring. Whatever the reason, it is the Lord who is seeking his own to return home to his faith community.

Nothing can separate us from the love of God. Many agonize over past failures and worry that they can't be forgiven. Jesus died for all of us and he set us free from sin. There is nothing we have done or that we can do that cannot be forgiven. We can always start over and change our lives for the better. It is the Lord who continually invites us to return to him and be transformed.

Lord, Jesus Christ,
thank you for seeking me out and
calling me to draw closer to you.
Fill my heart with your love,
banish all fear and darkness and
shield me from all harm.

Chapter Two

Life's Journey Has Many Twists and Turns

✎

Then Jesus said, "There was a man who had two sons. The younger of them said to his father, 'Father, give me the share of the property that will belong to me.' So he divided his property between them. A few days later the younger son gathered all he had and traveled to a distant country, and there he squandered his property in dissolute living. When he had spent everything, a severe famine took place throughout that country, and he began to be in need. So he went and hired himself out to one of the citizens of that country, who sent him to his fields to feed the pigs. He would gladly have filled himself with the pods that the pigs were eating; and no one gave him anything. But when he came to himself he said, 'How many of my father's

*hired hands have bread enough to spare,
but here I am dying of hunger! I will get up
and go to my father, and I will say to him,
"Father, I have sinned against heaven and
before you; I am no longer worthy to be
called your son; treat me like one of your
hired hands."' So he set off and went to his
father. But while he was still far off, his
father saw him and was filled with compassion;
he ran and put his arms around him and
kissed him. Then the son said to him, 'Father,
I have sinned against heaven and before you;
I am no longer worthy to be called your
son.' But the father said to his slaves, 'Quickly,
bring out a robe—the best one—and put it
on him; put a ring on his finger and sandals
on his feet. And get the fatted calf and kill
it, and let us eat and celebrate; for this son
of mine was dead and is alive again; he was
lost and is found!' And they began to celebrate.*

LUKE 15:11–24

∞∞∞

Prayer of a Seeker

*My God, I have no idea where I am going. I
do not see the road ahead of me. I cannot*

know for certain where it will end, and the fact that I think I am following your will does not mean that I am actually doing so.

But I believe that the desire to please you does in fact please you. And I hope I have that desire in all that I am doing. I hope that I will never do anything apart from that desire.

And I know that if I do this you will lead me by the right road, though I may know nothing about it. Therefore, I will trust you always and everywhere though I may seem to be lost in the shadow of death. I will not fear because you are ever with me and you will never leave me to face my perils alone.

This prayer just given is particularly relevant and apropos for Catholics who have drifted away from the Church. It seems to speak to our hearts and souls about the desolation, isolation, and loneliness of being separated from our faith community. Yet many of us who have been away from the Church speak of our certainty and even our sure knowledge that God was with us every step of the way during our absence from the Church! Jesus, the Good

Shepherd, walked with us and guided us even when we were not aware of his presence.

Most people drift away from their Catholic faith to one degree or another while growing up, maturing, and establishing their own families. Many eventually want to return. Some were never solidly connected in the first place. In today's highly mobile society, many people move so often that they never really put down roots in one location and never really connect with a Catholic parish or the Catholic faith. Often, registering at the local parish after moving into a new area is not a high priority; thus forming a connection with a Catholic parish becomes lost in the shuffle.

As part of the maturing process, young people need to establish their own personalities and individuality rather than relying solely on their parents for life direction and guidance. Frequently, this march toward maturation can be a painful and awkward process. For some young people, leaving the Catholic Church is an assertion of independence from their parents and a normal part of development toward maturity. Many parents have great difficulty letting their children grow up and make their own decisions, especially about religion. Frequently,

parents nag, badger, and hound their children—
even far into their adult lives—to get them to
attend a Catholic church. This strategy never
works and, in fact, has the opposite effect: many
people purposely stop attending the Catholic
Church just because their parents constantly
harp at them to do so.

Many people who have drifted away from the
Church say they never lost their faith in God,
only in the Catholic Church. The Church isn't
made up of angels, but rather sinful, weak human beings (who are just like everybody else!)
who make lots and lots of mistakes, some worse,
some not so bad. However, we always have room
for a few more sinners to join our faith community. None of us is perfect, and neither is our
Catholic Church community. Strive as we
might, most of us will not achieve formal saint-
hood. We are all sinners in need of healing and
repentance. We are the Church, a community
of broken, sinful disciples striving to do better.
However, we are also a community of faith-filled
disciples who pray for, nurture, and support one
another during life's ups and downs. It's tough
to journey through the hardships of life without the support of a loving and supportive faith
community.

Recently, a couple in their thirties started attending a Catholics Returning Home program at their parish after noticing the publicity in their community newspaper. They said they had successful careers and were making plenty of money but felt empty, unfulfilled, and adrift by not being rooted in their Catholic faith. In addition, they shared their frustrations concerning their failure to have children. They said they weren't expecting a miracle but just wanted support to help them accept life's disappointments. They faithfully attended for the duration of the six-week series and they joined our parish. A few months later at the next six-week Catholics Returning Home series, the young couple came back bubbling over with joy and announced that they were expecting a new baby. They were excited to share the announcement of this miracle with their new faith community.

A woman in her fifties returned a few years ago through a Catholics Returning Home program after she had just buried her only child. She had been away from formal Church membership for over thirty years because she said God gave her an only child who was severely physically disabled. She was devastated and grieving over the death of her only child, having endured years of anguish and grief over caring for her child who suffered from grave disabilities.

To make matters worse, she had been widowed twice. Her first husband and the father of her child died unexpectedly at a young age. She had remarried, but her second husband also died. During her years of grieving and attempting to care for her disabled child, she felt as though the Church and God had abandoned her. She didn't know where to turn. She felt that the people she interacted with in the Catholic Church were insensitive and uncaring toward her during her hardships. She found this especially true during the planning and arranging of all the funerals. During these events, she felt powerless and disenfranchised.

During the six weeks of a Catholics Returning Home program, she shared her grief and anger and gradually gained more trust and a feeling of belonging to the Catholic faith community. She liked the first six-week series so much that she came back for the next series as part of a preparation to help others return. The timing was near the anniversary of her daughter's death and she shared with us that she was going to have a special Mass said.

A few weeks later, she came in absolutely

beaming, radiant and confident, and asked to share a major milestone and accomplishment in her faith journey with us. She said before she attended the special anniversary Mass for her deceased daughter, she had purchased a rose and got permission from the priest-celebrant to put the rose on the altar before the Mass. She said that when she laid the rose on the altar, a sacristan at the parish told her very sternly and emphatically that she couldn't put that rose on the altar and that she must remove it. She said at first she felt crushed, humiliated, and demoralized and was going to remove the rose, leave the church, and never come back. But then she felt an overwhelming sense of confidence that she was in *her church* and no one was going to keep her from commemorating her deceased daughter. So she stood her ground and told the sacristan that the rose was for her beloved daughter, that she had got permission from the priest-celebrant to place the rose on the altar, that the Mass was being said for her daughter, and that this was her church. Furthermore, she said, the rose was staying right there on the altar. She said the sacristan was quite surprised and startled by her boldness, and backed down and left her be. She had prevailed! She said she

will never allow anyone else to drive her away
from her Catholic faith and her Church. The
others in her Catholics Returning Home group
clapped and congratulated her on her confidence, assertiveness, and on her taking owner-
ship and responsibility for her faith.

Your Catholic faith belongs to you, and no
one can take it from you. You are important,
missed, and part of our Catholic faith community. Just because you've been away from the
Church for a while doesn't mean that you're less
important or have a lower status than others in
the community. In the parable of the Prodigal
Son, when the son left, squandered his share of
his inheritance, and lived a loose life of sin, on
his return—when he was still "a long way off"—
his forgiving father met him, threw him a huge
party, and fully restored him to his place in the
family. In the same way, on returning home to your
Catholic faith, you can rejoin your faith community and reclaim your baptismal heritage.

Our God is a forgiving father, not one who
carries grudges or who is resentful. If you are
feeling overwhelming guilt for being away, it is
best to acknowledge that guilt, try to make
amends, and concentrate on doing better in the
future rather than staying stuck in the mistakes

of the past. The beauty of our Catholic faith is that you can be forgiven and start over with a clean slate to make improvements in your life. It is Jesus, the Good Shepherd, who is calling you to return, and he is willing to leave all the others in the community to seek you out and welcome you back. Be assured that he will care for you, guide you, and go before you to show you the way. Keep your focus on Jesus your shepherd instead of on others who would deter and discourage you by their sinfulness and failures. Remember that the Church is made up of ordinary, garden-variety sinners who are trying to do better. If the Church allowed only angels or perfect people to become members, none of us would be able to join!

Where can I flee
from your spirit, O Lord,
because you are always with us
even when we seem to be lost
and far from home.
Lead me, guide me,
protect me from all harm
because you alone,
O Lord, have the words
of eternal life.

Chapter Three

Where to Start and How to Reconnect
(Choosing a Parish, How to Register)

∽∾∾

[Jesus] also told this parable to some who trusted in themselves that they were righteous and regarded others with contempt: "Two men went up to the temple to pray, one a Pharisee and the other a tax collector. The Pharisee, standing by himself, was praying thus, 'God, I thank you that I am not like other people: thieves, rogues, adulterers, or even like this tax collector. I fast twice a week; I give a tenth of all my income.' But the tax collector, standing far off, would not even look up to heaven, but was beating his breast and saying, 'God, be merciful to me, a sinner!' I tell you, this man went down to his home justified rather than the

other; for all who exalt themselves will be humbled, but all who humble themselves will be exalted."

LUKE 18:9–14

∾

I f you have been away from the Catholic Church for a while, returning can be very frightening. Many folks are afraid to approach the Church for fear of being rejected. Some are unable to get up the nerve even to get out of their cars as they sit in the parking lot in front of the church or rectory instead of coming in. Many who walk in the doors after a long absence are shaking with fear. Right now, you may be wondering about your own status in the Church, and you might be feeling guilty for being away. Don't be afraid, because you indeed are welcome.

If you have any doubts, remember the poor tax collector who returned to the temple to pray but who was afraid and kept his distance, "not even daring to raise his eyes to heaven," and instead asked God for mercy from afar. But the tax collector was justified and received God's favor and forgiveness compared to the judgmental Pharisee who didn't even bow his head and instead self-righteously ridiculed the tax collector for being such a big sinner. The Lord sees your sincerity of heart and repentance and is pleased—that is all that counts. It really doesn't matter what others think or if they judge you. Let those who would judge you read the above parable and see where they fit in. Think about which position you would rather be in, that of the judgmental Pharisee or the repentant tax collector.

Keep in mind that if you left many years ago when you were in high school or college (and especially if you left before Vatican II), the Church is going to look a whole lot different, especially if you come back as an adult after an absence of many years. You may be fearful that you will not fit in because much about the Church has changed and isn't what you remember. There's no need to worry about your lack of knowledge or familiarity. Instead, you will find that many others in the Church are in the same situation; they are also seeking a better understanding of their Catholic faith. The truth is that most Catholic faith communities are so large that their members may not even notice newcomers—giving you the opportunity to blend in and stay anonymous if you like. The Lord and the angels in heaven know you're there, and that's what is most important. After all, it is the Lord who is the Good Shepherd; he has sought you out and called you to return.

You can check the Yellow Pages in a telephone book to find Roman Catholic parishes in your area. Until you feel comfortable at a parish, you don't need to register. Perhaps you will feel more comfortable by being anonymous until you feel ready to "put down roots" by registering. To register, you can call the parish office to find out what their requirements are. Some parishes register parishioners after Sunday Masses while others allow you to register over the phone. Usually the registration form asks for your name, address, family members, and basic information about what sacraments you've received. Some registration forms also give you options to volunteer your time in various ministries. To keep the parish vibrant and active, all are encouraged to volunteer their time, treasure, and talent so that the various ministries are staffed. In a typical parish community, most of the parish ministries are staffed by volunteers. Some larger parishes have paid staff, but most of the smaller parishes most likely do not.

Take your time about volunteering; you should first concentrate on getting comfortable and updated with your Catholic faith. Sometimes volunteering for various ministries can help you feel that you belong, but choose carefully so that you're not overwhelmed. Most parishes are constantly searching for volunteers to staff the various ministries, so opportunities to invest your time and talents will never be in short supply.

When inquiring about Catholic parishes, ask if they have special ministries for reaching out to inactive or nonpracticing Catholics. You can also call your diocesan office or check their Web site to find out if such ministries are available. There are plenty of ways of approaching and getting information that allow you to remain anonymous if you prefer. In addition, lots of people make inquiries on behalf of others, such as their children, other relatives, and friends, so that you can easily blend in if you like.

In some parts of the country, parishes restrict membership to people who live within the parish's geographic boundaries. Usually this is in areas of rapid growth where there is a need to limit the number of registered parishioners due to space limitations. Many parishes across the country do not have any geographic restrictions in order to register. Generally, you are free to attend the Catholic parish of your choice. Thus, shop around and select a Catholic parish where you feel welcome and comfortable.

Each parish community is different based on the makeup of the parishioners, and they all have a different array of ministries. For example, the music ministries come in all different styles. Some parishes have very accomplished choirs and instrumental backup while others are quite simple and informal. It all depends on the diversity, talents, and gifts of the people representing that particular faith community.

You're free to choose a parish that best fits your preferences. Don't allow your dislike of one particular Catholic parish to stop you from returning to your Catholic faith. Instead, find a Catholic parish where you feel at home and welcome. That is the beauty of our Catholic faith—we are fortunate to have many wonderful and diverse parishes to choose from.

Keep in mind that after you have gotten up your nerve to call or visit a parish, it's very possible and in fact quite likely that you may encounter someone who is busy and doesn't have much time to talk with you. It's not that you don't deserve the attention. Unfortunately, many parishes are short staffed and run by a variety of volunteers and have limited paid staff. Some parishes have teens staff the parish office and answer the phones to learn about volunteering and helping others. Teens usually have a lot of energy, enthusiasm, and good intentions; however, they're kids who haven't developed a lot of judgment and discretion. It takes a lot of different people to staff a parish, operate all the ministries, and affirm the members, so keep in mind that most parish workers are volunteers doing their best to serve their parish and the Lord with the limited time they have to offer.

If you have never been involved with the inner workings of a Catholic parish, you may have the opinion that the operations are similar to being associated with a large, well-run corporate business. Nothing could be further from the truth. Catholic parishes are more like a big, ongoing, and continuous multifamily reunion that is run by and held together by the good will and love shared among the family members. Conflicts occur regularly, numerous mistakes are made, and hopefully everybody learns a lot about tolerance and forgiveness toward one another. Isn't that what families are about? Why would a parish family be any different?

A few years ago in January, on the night my husband and I were slated to start our Catholic Returning Home program, we were bombarded with a howling blizzard. As the day wore on and the snow piled up, we were considering not even showing up to start our new series. Since we were the leaders, however, we felt we at least had to show up, so we cautiously drove to the parish. My husband brought along a shovel which he immediately put to use to clear a path so that we could get into the church. After we dug our way inside, we ticked off the remaining time so we could turn around and go home. Suddenly, a large four-wheel drive vehicle pulled up to the door. Four people climbed out and found their way to our meeting room. One of the couples were active Catholics and had driven their four-wheeler all the way to another suburb and back, about a seventy mile round trip in the blizzard, to bring their good friends who had been away from the Church for over thirty years to our Catholics Returning Home series. We, of course, stayed for the evening and were glad to welcome them back. The Catholic couple returned each week to help their friends feel comfortable about returning to the Church—a decision which they made at the end of the series. What a testament of friendship and love.

Last January while I was leading a Catholics Returning Home program at a parish in Wisconsin, I began the first evening by telling attendees that I knew it took a lot of courage for them to walk in the door after being away from the Church for so long. I told them that I knew how afraid they were because I, too, was in the same boat not so many years ago as I sat in my car in the church parking lot, afraid to come in. Immediately, one of the attendees, a big, strapping man in his late thirties, voiced his agreement. He said that he had done a lot of difficult and challenging things in his life (he'd earned a doctorate in math and worked as a teacher), but one of the most difficult things he'd ever done occurred earlier that evening when he and his wife arrived at the church parking lot. Just as I had done years before, they almost left as they tried to get up their nerve to come in rather than turn around and go back home.

Some years back, a middle-aged, well-dressed, very articulate lawyer attended our Catholics Returning Home series. He was quite angry and distant. He dazzled us with his command of the English language as he grabbed every opportunity to argue about every conceivable topic on which he could squeeze in an opinion edgewise. But he faithfully attended every week and, toward the end of the series, he gradually started opening up and sharing without incessantly arguing. One evening, he burst into tears and sobbed as he told us that he had been away from the Church since high school. His departure came as a result of being denied the privilege of wearing his school's athletic jacket because he was unjustly accused of some infraction of the school rules. He told us how humiliated and shamed he felt at being unfairly stripped of the right to wear the school jacket. He said he never got over the pain and humiliation of this high-school experience and was never able to attend a Catholic church since. However, after sharing his anguish and pain with our group, he was finally able to let his resentment go, and with this release of pain and resentment, he joined the parish after completing our Catholics Returning Home series.

A school superintendent and his wife attended one of our programs. They had been away from the Church for over twenty-five years. They couldn't recall all the details of the reasons for their exit, but their feelings were hurt when one of their children was ill and they felt their parish and priest was insensitive toward their needs. In the initial phase of the six-week Catholics Returning Home series, they were quite hostile and defensive. However, as they shared their disappointment, anger, and pain, they were able to find peace and comfort within the group. Toward the end of the program, they lamented over how much they had missed during all the years they hadn't attended church— and all over a rather insignificant disagreement.

Being separated from your faith community can be very lonely, especially during life's crisis periods. Human beings are social creatures and are meant to live in communities rather than in isolation. One of the harshest punishments for prisoners is solitary confinement because human beings are not built to be isolated and alone. No wonder Jesus, the Good Shepherd, would leave the ninety-nine to seek out the one who has wandered away from the others.

Show me the way, O Lord!
Light up my path,
keep me in your presence
and fill my life
with your wondrous,
healing love.

Chapter Four

What the Church Is Like Now

∽◦∾

"You are the light of the world. A city built on a hill cannot be hid. No one after lighting a lamp puts it under the bushel basket, but on the lampstand, and it gives light to all in the house. In the same way, let your light shine before others, so that they may see your good works and give glory to your Father in heaven."

MATTHEW 5:14–16

"In everything do to others as you would have them do to you; for this is the law and the prophets."

MATTHEW 7:12

Be merciful, just as your Father is merciful.
"Do not judge, and you will not be judged; do not condemn, and you will not

be condemned. Forgive, and you will be forgiven; give, and it will be given to you. A good measure, pressed down, shaken together, running over, will be put into your lap; for the measure you give will be the measure you get back."

LUKE 6:36-38

T oday's Catholic parish is a diverse community of disciples with a multitude of ministries from those sponsoring Bible study to those running soup kitchens. In Mother Teresa's words, we are the hands and feet of Jesus in the world. Prior to the Second Vatican Council (held in the early sixties), Catholic parishes were primarily staffed by priests and sisters with limited lay involvement. "Father" and "Sister" did almost everything. The Second Vatican Council was a worldwide meeting called by Pope John XXIII. All the Catholic bishops attended this council, at which they updated many of the Church's practices and customs. However, the basic tenets of Catholicism did not change.

Some people left the Catholic Church because

of the changes legislated by Vatican II, and others left because they felt the Church hadn't changed and modernized fast enough. Some of the more noticeable changes after Vatican II include the celebrating of Mass in English, the local language, instead of Latin, and receiving Communion under the form of both bread and wine. In most dioceses across the United States, there are periodic Latin Masses held for those who still wish to attend.

Most Catholic parishes have a priest as a pastor and one or more associate pastors and very few sisters, if any. In addition, many parishes have paid professional staffs, deacons, and a host of volunteers involved in a variety of ministries. Because of the priest shortage, some parishes don't have a full-time pastor. Instead, a priest may serve a group of parishes and travel between locations.

After Vatican II, the permanent diaconate was restored to the Church. Deacons are not priests, but are ordained men who can be married. Often their wives also are involved in parish ministry. The role of the deacon is to be of service, for example, to the homebound and sick of the parish or in catechetical (that is, teaching the faith) roles. Deacons can also perform marriages, baptisms, and funeral services; and sometimes they preach homilies. Many parishes have one or more deacons who assist the pastor. There are also a variety of paid professional positions such as pastoral associates and directors of religious and adult education. The number of paid professional staff depends on the size and resources of a particular parish. Most small or rural parishes have limited professional staff. Almost all parishes have a multitude of volunteer staff and workers who participate in many different ways.

The typical administrative structure of a parish has a priest as the pastor with an advisory parish council made up of volunteer lay people. The various ministries report to the parish council and are sometimes divided into by commissions, such as peace and justice, education, liturgy (Mass), and evangelization. Many parishes have grade schools, and all have religious and adult education programs. All of the various ministries rely heavily on volunteers to accomplish their mission.

Since many of us left the Church as teens or young adults, we have a limited understanding of our Catholic faith. Our faith formation and development should be a lifelong process. Fortunately, there are numerous opportunities for adult religious education and a multitude of support groups available. Many parishes work together cooperatively as a cluster or at the arch/diocesan level to offer various programs, such as outreach to nonpracticing Catholics and support for the divorced and remarried, including offering classes on annulments. You can get information about the ministries and classes available from the parish bulletin, Web site, or by calling the parish office.

The liturgy commission within a parish prepares the setting and music for the Masses. Usually, they're involved with decorating the church for the different seasons and special occasions. They may also write the "Prayers of the Faithful": these are the intercessions prayed during Mass, that is, when we recite a request or a need and then say "pray for us." Volunteer lectors do the reading of the Bible passages, and eucharistic ministers help the priest distribute Communion. All these different parish functions are always looking for volunteers to participate. Often they offer training to help get people started. Ushers are volunteers, and the music ministry is primarily volunteer, though many organists are now paid, and many choir directors and cantors are as well. Music in church is becoming more and more professional. Many parishes have a bereavement ministry that may include the arrangements for funeral Masses and follow-up support for the family.

The religious education of children is a primary activity in all parishes regardless of whether they have a school or not. Most children do not attend a Catholic school and instead attend religious education classes. One of the few paid positions in the parish might be the Director of Religious Education (DRE). Even so, probably all of the religious education teachers from first grade to high school are volunteers. They do receive training and formation but all of them are freely giving their time and talent to serve the parish and the Lord. Many of these dedicated people have jobs, families, and other commitments but they're taking time out of their busy lives to share their faith with the children and young people of their parish. Parents are the primary educators of their children and they need to take active responsibility to pass on the Catholic faith to their children. When parents participate in their children's religious education, it becomes much more meaningful and memorable to the child and has a much better chance of having a lifelong effect.

An unavoidable fact is that keeping all the ministries operating in an active parish takes lots of time, treasure, and talent from good-hearted and generous souls. Even at the risk of alienating those who do not like being asked for donations, the Church must ask for financial support. We live in a temporal world where the church needs a roof over parishioners heads and heat and lights in the buildings. God's grace is free, but we need to pay for and maintain the plumbing to get it here. It's a matter of personal responsibility and conscience to look prayerfully at our own situation and finances and determine how we can share our time, treasure, and talents with our parish. It's always a balance and requires prayerful discernment.

Some people go overboard on "doing for the Church" to the neglect of their personal and family responsibilities. Ideally, we need to carefully balance all of our responsibilities when determining our level and type of parish activity. "Doing good for the church" becomes bad when it is harmful or neglectful to your personal or family needs, as shown in the following story. A father with five young children moved out of his house and in with a lay religious community. His wife succeeded in getting him to call me and I talked with him at length, telling him I thought Jesus wouldn't want him to abandon his wife and five children. He emphatically disagreed, misquoting scriptural references to support his views. I would regularly get separate phone calls from both him and his wife, each maintaining their respective positions. The phones calls stopped, and for a time I didn't know what happened. I happened to attend a Sunday Mass at this couple's parish and as I got out of the car in the church parking lot I encountered the couple and their five children. The husband looked at me apologetically and told me that he finally realized that he did belong with his family, and that this was the first time he attend Mass with his family for months.

A few years ago I got a call from a man who said he was thinking about leaving the Church because of all the "clowns on the altar." I was completely baffled as to what he was talking about and so I asked him what Mass he was attending. He told me and it turned out to be the same Mass that I attended! I said that I had never noticed any clowns. He said he meant the lay lectors and eucharistic ministers who were defiling the altar. He said he wouldn't receive Communion from any unworthy, sinful clown and instead got in the line where the priest was distributing. His message finally clicked after the few seconds it took for me to get the image of clowns on the altar out of my head. I told him that since I was one of those clowns, being that I was both a lector and eucharistic minister, most likely I wasn't going to be much help to him. He agreed and angrily hung up on me.

A woman in her sixties attended a few weeks of a Catholics Returning Home program after being away from the Church since high school. However, she did not return for the full series of meetings. When I called to find out how she was doing she said that she had left because the Church was filled with hypocrites, and it looked like not much had changed. I suggested that if she didn't like our parish she might try some of the others in the area. She promptly retorted that the other parishes were probably just a bunch of hypocrites, too. I agreed with her that the Catholic Church is filled with hypocrites and sinners, but I also told her that we always have room for a few more if she ever changes her mind and cares to join us.

Our Catholic community is made up of all different kinds of sinners and hypocrites because we are part of humanity and we are in constant need of conversion, repentance, and forgiveness. Jesus came into the world to save sinners, not the self-righteous. Saints are sinners who just keep trying to do better. Thus, we're on a life-long journey together toward God, trying to overcome our human weakness, sinfulness, and failures one day at a time. Our Catholic faith community helps and supports us on our life's journey toward wholeness and holiness. We believe that you too could find comfort and support within our faith community and we invite you to join us.

Have mercy on me, O God,
according to your steadfast love;
according to your abundant mercy,
blot out my transgressions.
Wash me thoroughly from my iniquity,
and cleanse me from my sin.
For I know my transgressions,
and my sin is ever before me….
Purge me with hyssop,
and I shall be clean;
wash me,
and I shall be whiter than snow.
Let me hear joy and gladness;

let the bones that you have
crushed rejoice.
Hide your face from my sins,
and blot out all my iniquities.
Create in me a clean heart, O God,
and put a new and right spirit
within me.

PSALM 51:1–3, 7–10

Chapter Five

Overview of the Mass, Reconciliation, and the Nicene Creed

∽∾∽

While they were eating, Jesus took a loaf of bread, and after blessing it he broke it, gave it to the disciples, and said, "Take, eat; this is my body." Then he took a cup, and after giving thanks he gave it to them, saying, "Drink from it, all of you; for this is my blood of the covenant, which is poured out for many for the forgiveness of sins."

MATTHEW 26:26–28

Then Peter came and said to him, "Lord, if another member of the church sins against me, how often should I forgive? As many as seven times?" Jesus said to him, "Not seven times, but, I tell you, seventy-seven times.

"For this reason the kingdom of heaven may be compared to a king who wished to settle accounts with his slaves. When he began the reckoning, one who owed him ten thousand talents was brought to him; and, as he could not pay, his lord ordered him to be sold, together with his wife and children and all his possessions, and payment to be made. So the slave fell on his knees before him, saying, 'Have patience with me, and I will pay you everything.' And out of pity for him, the lord of that slave released him and forgave him the debt. But that same slave, as he went out, came upon one of his fellow slaves who owed him a hundred denarii; and seizing him by the throat, he said, 'Pay what you owe.' Then his fellow slave fell down and pleaded with him, 'Have patience with me, and I will pay you.' But he refused; then he went and threw him into prison until he would pay the debt. When his fellow slaves saw what had happened, they were greatly distressed, and they went and reported to their lord all that had taken place. Then his lord summoned him and said to him, 'You wicked slave! I forgave you all that

*debt because you pleaded with me. Should
you not have had mercy on your fellow
slave, as I had mercy on you?' And in anger
his lord handed him over to be tortured
until he would pay his entire debt. So my
heavenly Father will also do to every one
of you, if you do not forgive your brother
or sister from your heart."*

MATTHEW 18:21–35

*One of them, a lawyer, asked him a question
to test him. "Teacher, which commandment
in the law is the greatest?" He said to him,
"'You shall love the Lord your God with
all your heart, and with all your soul, and
with all your mind.' This is the greatest
and first commandment. And a second is
like it: 'You shall love your neighbor as
yourself.' On these two commandments
hang all the law and the prophets."*

MATTHEW 22:35–40

The Mass

For Catholics, celebrating Eucharist together is central to the practice of our faith. No matter how long it's been since we've last attended Mass, we never seem to get over yearning for our eucharistic celebration. Something is missing even if we attend faith services of a different denomination. It's the symbolism and imagery of the candles, stained-glass windows, incense, artwork, music, Bible readings, and homily. But, mostly, it's the peacefulness and joy of sharing Eucharist with our loving faith community that profoundly touches our hearts and souls.

Attending Mass after a long absence is usually a peak emotional experience for many and frequently evokes a tearful response. Many have told me they can't stop crying every time they attend Mass. There are many styles and methods of individual prayer from reflective reading to silent contemplation. Tears of joy and thanksgiving are really heartfelt and spontaneous prayers offered to God for bringing you safely back home to your Catholic faith community. Be assured that Jesus, the Good Shepherd, sees your sincerity of heart and joyfully accepts your tears as precious gifts offered out of love.

The Church year is different from our calendar year and revolves around the events in Jesus' life. Each part of the Church year is signified by different colors, for example, green is used during Ordinary Time and violet is used during Advent. Different vestment colors may be used for the various types of liturgies, such as the feast day of martyrs in contrast to a celebration of the Blessed Mother.

Jesus celebrated the Eucharist for the first time on Holy Thursday, the night before he was crucified on Good Friday. Each year on Holy Thursday, we commemorate the Last Supper and the first Eucharist. The order of the Mass begins with the introductory rites. These include an entrance song and procession, a greeting, the penitential rite, sometimes the *Gloria*, and an opening prayer.

We come to Mass to join with our sisters and brothers as the one Body of Christ. The entrance song gives us our first opportunity to pray *together*, all of us using the same words. The procession by the priest and other ministers represents us coming from our various walks of life to approach the altar for this celebration. The Church teaches that Christ is really present among us "where two or three are gathered" in his name (Mt 18:20). So through the greeting, we recognize that presence of Christ in each other. During the penitential rite, the priest-celebrant invites the congregation to recall God's great mercy in having called us to celebrate the Eucharist. In the *Gloria* we give praise to God. Finally, the priest says, "Let us pray," and there is a moment of silence for all to pray. He then gathers all our personal prayers and offers them to God in the "opening prayer."

Next is the Liturgy of the Word. This includes readings from the Bible, a homily, the profession of faith, and the prayers of the faithful (or intercessions). We believe that when the Scriptures are proclaimed aloud before an assembly of people, it is God speaking directly to us today. That is why each Scripture passage read concludes with the phrase, "The Word of the Lord." The Church teaches that such a public proclamation of Scripture is another way the "real presence" of Christ comes to us.

In the homily, the priest-celebrant talks about how the readings relate to living out our Catholic faith in daily life. The profession of faith involves the recitation of the Nicene Creed (or the Apostles' Creed) and is the basis and summary of our Catholic beliefs. (A section-by-

section explanation of the Nicene Creed is pro-
vided at the end of this chapter.) Thus, at each
Sunday Mass, we recite and reaffirm our basic
Catholic beliefs.

The Liturgy of the Eucharist is the next part
of the Mass and it includes the preparation of
the altar and gifts, a eucharistic prayer, and the
Communion rite which includes the Lord's
Prayer, the sign of peace, and the sharing of holy
Communion.

In the first of these rituals, we bring the fruits
of the earth and of human labor to offer them
to God in heaven, just as did the people in the
Old Testament. This offering is symbolized by
the bread (made from wheat) and the wine
(made from grapes). Usually, the collection of
money is also done at this time for the support
of the parish, it ministries, and for the poor.
During the eucharistic prayer (there are now
several the priest can choose from), those gifts
of bread and wine are transformed into the body
and blood of Christ. We then offer the body of
God's Son, present here on the altar, to the Father, just as he was offered on the cross so long
ago. And think about it, the gift of one's own
child has to be the greatest gift we can possibly
offer to any parent—even to God. And since

through our baptism we have become members of Christ's body, we are also offering ourselves at the same time.

We pray the Lord's Prayer because it's the prayer Jesus himself taught us (Mt 6:9). Just as Christ has now become present on the altar, bringing with him peace for the world, we share with one another his peace. And then we each approach the altar as another affirmation of our belief in God's presence. By receiving Communion, we become intimately united with God and with one another as the body of Christ, and we renew and deepen our own position as a member of Christ's body.

The concluding rite includes the blessing and dismissal of the gathering. The blessing gives us extra spiritual strength to go about our daily work, and the dismissal reminds us that we have a mission to carry out in the world: "Go in peace, *to love and serve the Lord.*"

Don't worry if you're not sure when you're supposed to sit, stand, or kneel during Mass; watch those beside you and follow what they do. Most parishes have seasonal missals in the pews that have the order of the Mass and the related scriptural readings which you can follow. Since the missals are discarded after they're used for the time period indicated, you can check with the parish office and ask if they'll give you some of the old missals so that you can read them and gain a better understanding of the order of the Mass. In addition, many parishes have various publications available that explain the Mass as well as other religious topics. For more information, Chapter 6 includes a resource list of Web sites and books on a variety of topics from reconciliation to an explanation of the Mass.

Reconciliation

If you have not been practicing your faith as a Catholic for a while, when you are ready, you will need to celebrate the sacrament of reconciliation (formerly known as "penance" or "confession"). This step will be an important one before you participate at Mass fully (that is, receive Communion or any of the other sacraments). For many returning Catholics, the thought of going to reconciliation after many years causes sheer terror and panic. Yet the newer approach to this sacrament is designated very well by the name we now call it: reconciliation.

Think about it like this: if you have ever been

estranged from a dear friend or family member for a long time, or if you have hurt someone through something you did or did not do, eventually you have to heal the breach in the relationship. We have to apologize, and then accept the other person's love once again in return.

That's what the sacrament of reconciliation is all about—apologizing for not living up to what we promised in baptism, and then basking in the acceptance and love of God and of every other member of this community we call church. It's like telling your mom you were sorry for doing something you weren't supposed to when you were a little kid, and then her saying to you, "That's okay; I still love you anyway." Sometimes it takes a lot of courage to admit that we are not as perfect as we would like others to think we are, but there is really no need to be afraid of going to see a priest for the sacrament of reconciliation.

You have a choice on where to go. You can go to your local parish, a neighboring parish, or any other facility, such as shrines that offer Masses and reconciliation. You can call and make an appointment beforehand or show up at the scheduled time that reconciliation is offered. There are reconciliation rooms where you can talk face to face with a priest or you can stay anonymous behind a screen if you prefer. Some parishes have cards available that outline the procedure and tell you how to celebrate the sacrament of reconciliation. If none are available, just tell the priest that you've been gone a long time and need help on what to do; he'll be happy to help you. The focus is no longer on laundry lists of sins and related punishments; instead, the focus is more on your life patterns and those attitudes that need improvement.

Many parishes have communal reconciliation services before Christmas and Easter that begin with scriptural readings, music, and communal prayer, followed by individual reconciliation offered afterward. Since we are all part of the Body of Christ, whenever we hurt God or someone else, we injure our relationship with the whole Body. Communal reconciliation services help us to be more aware that our personal faults and sins affect other people, too.

Many returning Catholics agonize over and put off celebrating the sacrament of reconciliation because they're afraid of being yelled at by the priest. If you're really worried about possibly getting yelled at, reread the parable about the merciless debtor who was forgiven much but in turn wouldn't forgive another for a smaller debt owed to him. All of us, including priests, are sinners and have fallen short of the mark many, many times. Despite these failings, Jesus calls us to forgive ourselves and others from the heart; otherwise we risk offending God by committing the sin of unforgiveness. Remember that God's mercy is bigger than all of our sins.

A significant stumbling block to returning to the Church and the sacrament of reconciliation is the question of remarriage after a divorce or desertion. The following story represents a typical case. I got a call from a man who had recently moved to Illinois from Texas. He said his neighbors gave him a flyer for a Catholics Returning Home program that was listed in their church bulletin. He had recently met his next-door neighbors and when they mentioned that their kids attended the local Catholic school, he told them he used to be Catholic. He had been away from the Church for over twenty years since his wife had left him and their children. He eventually met and married another woman who helped him raise his children. He said he knew he could no longer be Catholic because he had remarried outside the Church. He said he loved his Catholic faith and remarked that the burden of not being able to be part of his Church was a constant source of sorrow and pain for him. He attended the Catholics Returning Home series, and we put him in touch with our pastoral associate who helped him through the annulment process so he was eventually married in the Church.

Annulments are not really new in the Church; they were just not used very much before Vatican Council II. The Church still teaches very strongly that a sacramental marriage is indissoluble, and so it does not allow divorce and remarriage. However, using the science of modern psychology, the Church recognizes that sometimes people get married who are not well suited for marriage for a variety of reasons. In such cases, the Church might judge that God did not bless a particular marriage as "sacramental," meaning that perhaps this marriage was not part of God's will.

The reasons for this might involve some psychological problem at the time of the marriage, immaturity, or a lack of freedom (for example, an arranged or "forced" marriage). For example, in days gone by, simply because a young couple accidentally got pregnant, they were often forced by society's standards to get married, even if they were not truly in love, or they were too young to accept the responsibility of family life. If such a couple later decided to separate because they could not work things out, the Church would consider annulling that marriage on grounds that they were not freely responding to God's love in their lives as is necessary for any sacrament. The marriage was still legal *and valid*, so any children it produced are legitimate. But the Church would declare that the marriage was not sacramental in the eyes of God, so the persons are free to marry in the Church again.

How do we know if a marriage was not a sacrament? Obviously, people cannot declare a marriage annulled on their own. Working with a priest, an individual (or a couple) petitions a special tribunal in their diocese who examines all the elements of the marriage and makes a judgment about it based on its findings. The process can be long and intrusive into one's personal life, but it can be worth going through to gain one's freedom to marry the person you really love and belong with.

A few years ago a highly educated woman with a Ph.D. in psychiatric social work attended a returning Catholics program after being away from the Church since college. She said she left because she outgrew the need for an outdated and superstitious institution that was oppressive toward women. During the session we were discussing the sacrament of reconciliation, this woman said the final incident that caused her to leave the Church involved this sacrament. She had gone to confession one day back in the sixties and the priest yelled at her and chastised her harshly for her failures. She said she would never go to confession again. More than three decades later, however, she was now changing her mind and decided that reconciliation could be a healing experience. Since she was absolutely petrified to go, she begged me to go with her. I helped her make an appointment with a priest and I went with her to meet the priest and waited outside. She, while ghost white and shaking like a leaf, went in. A short time later, she came out beaming, smiling ear to ear. She said she felt like a new person.

It's always a relief if we're able to get rid of the negative baggage we're carrying. Jesus, our Good Shepherd, is willing to take our burdens onto himself and lighten our load. What a priceless treasure and source of comfort we have in him! If you are weighed down with many burdens and failures and are seeking relief and comfort, turn to Jesus with confidence. To help you collect your thoughts as you reflect on your past, read and consider the sample examination of conscience at the end of this chapter. Ask Jesus for strength and guidance as you continue your journey back to your Catholic faith. Be assured that he will lead you on the right path every step of the way.

Bless the LORD, O my soul,
and all that is within me,
bless his holy name.
Bless the LORD, O my soul,
and do not forget
all his benefits—
who forgives all your iniquity,
who heals all your diseases,
who redeems your life from the Pit,
who crowns you with steadfast
love and mercy,
who satisfies you with good
as long as you live....

PSALM 103:1-5

Examination of Conscience

Prior to participating in the sacrament of reconciliation, it can be helpful to reflect on one's
life by asking certain questions of one's self.
These questions regarding your relationship
with yourself, your neighbor, and God can assist
you in expressing to your confessor (the priest)
those areas in your life that require God's grace
and mercy.

∽∼∾

Am I at peace with myself?

Am I honest with myself at all times?
Am I patient with myself?
Do I brood over my failings?
Have I forgiven myself for my sins and
    shortcomings?
Am I still growing, developing?
Am I set in my ways, unwilling to change?
Do I take care of myself? Physically?
    Spiritually?

Am I at peace with others?

What disrupts the harmony that should exist between myself and…

My spouse?
My children?
My parents?
My relatives?
My friends?
My neighbors?

Do I deal justly with others, giving them what is due them:

My employers?
My employees?
My fellow workers?

Am I at peace with God?

What disrupts the harmony he wants to exists between us?
Do I see God as a lawgiver and judge or as a loving, merciful Savior?
Have I allowed other things or persons to take his place in my life?
Have I thanked him for his endless compassion and limitless love?

Am I at peace with the world?

Do I see the world as something given to
me and all persons that will come
after me as a trust?

Have I abused its resources?

Am I wasteful: With money? With the
things I use? With my time? With
others' time?

Must I always have the latest? The best?

Do I feel responsibility for my community?

Do I vote? Have I volunteered to help?

> *Lord, Jesus Christ,*
> *Son of God,*
> *have Mercy on me,*
> *a sinner.*

∽

The Nicene Creed

The Nicene Creed was originally formulated
at the First Ecumenical Council of the Catholic
Church held in Nicea in A.D. 325 and was
later amplified, adopted, and authorized as a
true expression of the Faith at the Second
Ecumenical Council in Constantinople in A.D.
381. Gradually, the Nicene Creed came to

be recognized as the proper profession of faith for candidates for the sacrament of baptism. It is the profession of the Christian Faith common to the Catholic Church.

Since the Creed is the basis of our Catholic faith, it's important that we grow in our understanding and appreciation of what it means instead of reciting it by rote like a parrot. A powerful exercise is to read each section along with the related explanation and think about what it means to your life. You will be surprised about what insights the Lord will reveal to you.

∽∾

We believe in one God,
the Father, the Almighty,
maker of heaven and earth,
of all that is, seen and unseen.

Explanation: *Ancient religions believed in different "gods" for different purposes. We believe there is only one God, who is all-powerful, and who created and cares for all things.*

We believe in one Lord, Jesus Christ,
the only Son of God
eternally begotten of the Father,
God from God, Light from Light,
true God from true God,
begotten, not made,
one in Being with the Father.
Through him all things were made.

Explanation: This part gets complicated with its rather heavy theology about exactly who Jesus Christ is. What it means is that Jesus Christ is the only "Lord" or "Messiah" or "Savior" we have. He is related to God the Father as his son, yet he is from all eternity, just like his Father. He also truly is God—not a creature—the same God as the Father (they are one being). In fact, he was there from the beginning and helped create everything.

For us and our salvation
he came down from heaven;
by the power of the Holy Spirit
he was born of the Virgin Mary,
and became man.

Explanation: Even though Jesus was God, out of love for us he chose to come share life on earth with us to save us; the Holy Spirit hovered over Mary, who was a virgin, and she miraculously became pregnant with Jesus. She was his earthly mother; the Holy Spirit is his heavenly father. That is how we know Jesus is both God and human.

For our sake he was crucified under Pontius Pilate;
he suffered, died, and was buried.
On the third day he rose again
in fulfillment of the Scriptures;
he ascended into heaven
and is seated at the right hand
of the Father.
He will come again in glory to judge
the living and the dead,
and his kingdom will have no end.

Explanation: *Jesus was hung on a tree for our sakes. He actually died and even was buried. But he came to life again three days later—a new kind of life, as was foretold in the Old Testament. Sometime after rising, his already glorified body went into heaven, where he now lives with the Father. At the end of time, he will come back to bring into heaven all good people who have ever lived. And they also will live with God forever.*

We believe in the Holy Spirit, the Lord,
the giver of life,
who proceeds from the Father and the Son.
With the Father and the Son he is worshiped
and glorified.
He has spoken through the Prophets.

Explanation: *The Holy Spirit is the third Person in the Trinity of the one being that makes up the mystery of God. The Holy Spirit shares its divine life with us. The Holy Spirit grows out of the infinite love the Father and Son have for each other. The Holy Spirit also is God, and so we adore the Holy Spirit, too. It is the Holy Spirit who inspired the writers of the Scriptures.*

We believe in one holy catholic and
apostolic Church.
We acknowledge one baptism for the
forgiveness of sins.
We look for the resurrection of the dead,
and the life of the world to come. Amen.

Explanation: *We believe in a Church that is united under the pope as its head; that is holy because God is present with it and within it; that is universal—meaning it is for everyone; and that has a mission to fulfill here on earth. We believe that the baptism of Jesus Christ is the only baptism that saves us from sin. And we have hope that someday we, too, will rise with Christ and live with him forever.*

Chapter Six

Resources: Books, Bulletins, Web Sites, and Groups

∽✌∾

God's Love and Truth

"For God so loved the world that he gave his only Son, so that everyone who believes in him may not perish but may have eternal life.

"Indeed, God did not send the Son into the world to condemn the world, but in order that the world might be saved through him…the light has come into the world, and people loved darkness rather than light because their deeds were evil. For all who do evil hate the light and do not come to the light, so that their deeds may not be exposed. But those who do what is true come to the light, so that it may be clearly seen that their deeds have been done in God."

JOHN 3:16–21

Jesus and the Children

People were bringing even infants to him that he might touch them; and when the disciples saw it, they sternly ordered them not to do it. But Jesus called for them and said, "Let the little children come to me, and do not stop them; for it is to such as these that the kingdom of God belongs. Truly I tell you, whoever does not receive the kingdom of God as a little child will never enter it."

LUKE 18:15–17

Jesus and His Father

At that time Jesus said, "I thank you, Father, Lord of heaven and earth, because you have hidden these things from the wise and the intelligent and have revealed them to infants...."

MATTHEW 11:25

∾

To seek the truth is to seek God. It is a grace from God to be open and seeking to know more about him. Many of us who were away from the Church had minimal religious education years ago when we were children. As adults, we may be well educated, highly trained and successful in our "day jobs," but we're still children in our understanding of our Catholic Christian faith. But, the reign of God belongs to those who accept the kingdom of God as a child. We're blessed that the Lord has called us to know him better.

Below is a listing of excellent resources to help us update our understanding of our Catholic Christian faith. A children's Bible, for children of all ages, is an excellent place to start. The stories are well written and easy to understand, the pictures are colorful and it's referenced to the regular Bible. If you are a parent or grandparent, you can read the stories to them and learn together. When you're ready to move to a higher level, you can easily get a regular adult Bible and it already will be very familiar to you. In addition, most parishes have Bible-study classes available. Our faith development and religious education is a life-long process. The more we learn about our faith, the more committed disciples we become.

Specific Books

Catechism of the Catholic Church, United States Catholic Conference, Doubleday, 1995.

Catholic Annulment: Spiritual Healing, Dennis and Kay Flowers, Liguori Publications, 2002.

Catholic Answers to Fundamentalists' Questions, Philip St. Romain, Liguori Publications, 1984.

A Children's Bible for Children of All Ages. This is available at most bookstores and Catholic publishers; it serves as an excellent overview of biblical teachings and is referenced to the Bible.

Faith for the Future: A New Illustrated Catechism, Liguori Publications, 1998.

The Gift of Sex: A Christian Guide to Sexual Fulfillment, Dr. Clifford and Joyce Penner, Penner Books and Tapes, Pasadena, Calif., 1981. Phone: 626/449-2525.

Handbook for Today's Catholics, A Redemptorist Pastoral Publication (also available in Spanish), Liguori Publications, 1994.

Loving Jesus, Mother Teresa, Servant Publications, Ann Arbor, Mich., 1991.

The Matter of Life and Death: Surviving Loss and Finding Hope, Msgr. Thomas Hartman with Joe Cook, Liguori Publications, 1994.

My Hope for the Church, Bernard Haring, C.Ss.R.,
Liguori Publications, 1999.

New Revised Standard Version Bible, copyright
1989 by the Division of Christian Education
of the National Council of the Churches
of Christ in the U.S.A.

A Sense of Sexuality: Christian Love and Intimacy,
Evelyn and James Whitehead, Cross Road,
1994.

A Time to Listen…A Time to Heal, USCCB,
Washington, D.C., 1998. A national directory
of programs designed to reach out to inactive/
nonpracticing Catholics.

*Vatican Council II: The Conciliar and Post
Conciliar Documents*, Austin Flannery, O.P.,
Costello Publishing Company, Northport,
New York, 1992.

*While You Were Gone: A Handbook For Returning
Catholics*, William J. Bausch, Twenty-Third
Publications, Mystic, Conn., 1994.

*Your Faith: A Popular Presentation of Catholic
Belief* (Revised Edition), A Redemptorist
Pastoral Publication, Liguori Publications,
2004.

Bulletins

Catholic Update articles on various topics by St. Anthony Messenger Press (1615 Republic Street, Cincinnati, OH 45210, Tel: 1-800-488-0488, http://www.catholicupdate.org).

Resource List of Specific Support Groups/Web Sites

American Association of Pastoral Counselors, 9504A Lee Highway, Fairfax, VA 22031-2303; Phone: 703-385-6967; http://www.AAPC.org. The AAPC provides and promotes theologically informed, spiritually sensitive, ethically sound, and clinically competent counseling and consultation as an extension of the ministry of faith communities. The AAPC is an excellent resource for those returnees in need of professional assistance in dealing with past hurts and future healing.

Once Catholic—A Catholic Site for Seekers, http://www.oncecatholic.org.

WEORC, 1528 West Glenlake, Chicago, IL 60660-1826; http//www.marriedpriests.org. A like-to-like ministry that provides counseling, support, and assistance in finding employment for former religious making the transition back to secular life.

Other Related Liguori Publications Titles

INVITING CATHOLICS HOME
A Parish Program
Sally L. Mews

This book is about "Catholics Returning Home," a six-week support program aimed to help Catholics return to the Church. The program's non-judgmental approach is designed to recognize each participant's feelings and help each to understand they are not alone. Program activities, suggestions for publicizing the program and recommendations for follow-up make this an effective evangelization resource.

ISBN 978-0-7648-0844-9

CATHOLICS CONTINUING THE JOURNEY
A Faith Sharing Program for Small Groups
Sally L. Mews

This six-week program, originally designed to help people grow in their faith after returning to the Church, is an excellent reflection tool for any study group in the parish setting. Each session lasts approximately 1-1/2 to 2 hours and follows the theme: "What is your image of Jesus?" It is an appropriate study course for any time of the year and its emphasis on group dynamics makes it an easy and effective way to build community among parishioners.

ISBN 978-0-7648-1503-4

HANDBOOK FOR TODAY'S CATHOLIC
Revised Edition

Handbook for Today's Catholic is presented in easy-to-understand language, with content divided into Beliefs, Practices, Prayers, and Living the Faith, and is also fully indexed to the *Catechism of the Catholic Church*. RCIA and parish adult faith formation groups, high school religious education classes, inquirers into the Catholic Faith, and anyone who wants to have the essentials of Catholicism at their fingertips will welcome this affordable faith resource.

ISBN 978-0-7648-1220-0

For prices and ordering information,
call us toll free at 800-325-9521
or visit our Web site, www.liguori.org.